Hector Ruiz

Calgary, July 20 2013

INDIAN Lemonade

It's a BIG little World

INDIAN Lemonade

Hector Larrazabal

Illustrated by Anna Tsocheva

ADVENTURES
NATION

Published in 2013 by
Adventures Nation
Calgary, Alberta, Canada
http://adventuresnation.com

Cataloguing data available from Library and Archives Canada

ISBN 978-0-9919619-0-0 (Hardback)
ISBN 978-0-9919619-1-7 (Paperback)
ISBN 978-0-9919619-2-4 (ePub)
ISBN 978-0-9919619-3-1 (Mobi)

*To every child who
dreams of exploring our
big little world*

Contents

About the It's a Big Little World Series

The *It's a Big Little World* series introduces children to the concept and challenges of globalization by combining travel, multiculturalism, and entrepreneurship in exciting, true-to-life scenarios. In this series, two North American children, Rocky and Allie, travel the world with their parents and have many an opportunity to learn about the culture and traditions of each country they visit.

As Rocky and Allie visit new countries, they make new friends and learn about cultural elements unique to each country or region. More importantly, Rocky, as an entrepreneur in the making, introduces his local hosts to business solutions as he himself becomes aware of his own need to adapt to a foreign cultural and social environment.

As the world we live in continues to evolve, globalization will continue to play an important role in new economic, social, and geopolitical developments. Globalization is affecting the lifestyles of people – especially children – in developing countries as new traditions are being imposed and are threatening to supplant local culture and reduce cultural diversity.

Books in the *It's a Big Little World* series highlight the need of children and their parents, wherever they live, to develop specific skills to preserve their own culture, traditions, and values and to accept those of other people as part of thriving in a globalized world.

Adaptability, effective communication, teamwork, and empathy are critical to maintaining an environment in which greater connectivity does not erode the cultural and social traditions of countries across our very big, and very little, world.

CHAPTER I

Incredible India

Today is a big day for my family. We're going to what my father calls a most incredible and fantastic place. That place is a country called India.

My sister and I are really excited to discover India, visit many interesting places, learn about the culture, and make many new friends.

My name is Rocky. I am eight years old. Allie, my sister, is one year younger than I am. And my dog, Bedoo, a miniature schnauzer, is two years old.

Allie and I are lucky because our dad runs an international business and has decided to take the whole family with him as he travels the world for work.

He explained we would be visiting many interesting and beautiful countries over the next several years as his company continues to grow.

Why does that make us lucky? Because it means lots of adventures for Allie and me – and for Bedoo, too.

India is a really big country. Its population is 1.2

billion people. That's almost four times the population of the United States. India's official currency is the rupee. India has many traditions, and its citizens speak many languages and dialects. My dad says the main language is Hindi.

"But you'll have no problem at all speaking to the people, playing with your new friends, and navigating the cities and towns we visit," he told Allie and me. "Most people in the big cities speak English."

The journey to India was a long one. We flew for almost an entire day and were really tired when we finally arrived. Allie was in better shape than I was. She slept for at least eight hours during the trip. I was so excited that I had just a few short naps.

We landed at Indira Gandhi International Airport in New Delhi, India's capital city. As soon as we landed, we knew we were in a very different place. The first thing I noticed was the big hand sculptures that seemed so real I thought they were reaching out to touch me.

"They are called mudras," my mom said. "I do these hand gestures to meditate when I practice yoga. The mudras help me relax when I'm stressed."

And so our adventures began, right from the moment we arrived!

The airport was big and crowded. We thought we were going to get lost in the sea of people.

Everyone was friendly. They were dressed in colorful outfits. The women wore a traditional Indian dress called a sari, and the men wore a tradi-

tional outfit called a kurta pajama. Allie was captivated by the beautiful saris and couldn't wait to try
one on and maybe own one, too.

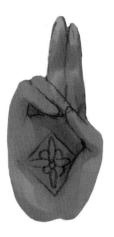

CHAPTER II

Our First Look at New Delhi

Once we got through the crowd at the airport, and the immigration agents had checked our passports, we headed to our new apartment in the middle of the city.

The streets were crowded, and the traffic was slow. We saw hundreds of little rickshaws – the ones that look like a bicycle with a big seat in the back for two passengers.

There were also many green and yellow cars. Our mother told us the people here call them auto rickshaws. They look almost like little toy cars. I, for one, couldn't wait to tour the city in one of them.

We saw big trucks and small motorcycles. The

trucks looked very different from the ones back home. They were painted in bright colors and decorated with lots of ornaments.

"It shows the drivers' pride in their vehicles," my dad said.

And the motorcycles didn't carry just one person. I couldn't believe it when I saw a whole family in one of them.

And that's not all. There were even some cows and elephants on the streets.

It was all a bit confusing, and a little frightening, but everyone looked happy and lively, and they smiled at us when they saw our faces through the car windows.

We could see that, beyond the busy and noisy streets, New Delhi was a beautiful city. On our way to our new apartment, we drove past several buildings and monuments.

I was really captivated by a big, tall monument.

"What is it?" I asked.

"It reminds me of the Arch of Triumph in Paris," my mother said.

Then my father added, imitating a history professor, "It is called India Gate. It commemorates the soldiers from the British Indian army who lost their lives in World War I."

From what I could see so far, I knew I was going to like New Delhi very much.

CHAPTER III
New Friends and New Adventures

A few weeks after we arrived in India, every-thing was still far from normal for our family. Allie and I were getting used to our new school, but we were homesick for our friends back home.

Luckily, everyone at school was very friendly. We knew that soon we would have lots of new friends.

And did we ever make lots of new friends! Tarun, a seven-year-old boy, and Neema, his eight-year-old sister, became our best friends in India. They lived near our apartment building. We were able to go back and forth to school with them every day.

They loved my dog Bedoo — so much that they even asked their parents to get a dog just like him.

The school was taught in English, but Allie and I learned some new words in Hindi from some of the boys and girls in our classes. Most of the students were children of businesspeople from other countries, but Tarun and Neema's parents weren't businesspeople. Their mother was a history teacher at our school, and their father was an engineer who worked for a large Indian company in the city.

Tarun and Neema showed us around our new neighborhood. They even took my sister to the market to try on lots of saris and scarves and to look at some jewelry, too. They also showed us the spice market and some important monuments in Old Delhi. We were impressed by the Red Fort, which was close to the market.

"The Red Fort was built in the seventeenth century by the Mughal Emperor Shah Jahan," Tarun said. "The Red Fort served as the residence of the Mughal Emperors when Shah Jahan moved the country's capital from the city of Agra to Old Delhi."

Tarun loved Indian history and was always eager to teach Allie and me.

After we walked around the market and admired the impressive Red Fort, we decided to continue touring the market in rickshaws. Tarun and Neema took one rickshaw, and Allie, Bedoo, and I got in another.

The market was huge. The smell of spices was strong, and so was the smell of food that was being prepared in the streets around the market. I could pick up the scents of cinnamon, cloves, and ginger my mom uses every time she bakes cookies.

Everything was crowded – so much so that Allie and I lost sight of Tarun and Neema.

What were we going to do now? How would we find them? Our rickshaw driver didn't speak any English.

I took out my tablet and tried to find a map to guide us back to the main street. It didn't matter, though. The map was useless because we couldn't see anything but rickshaws and the crowd of people ahead of us.

Luckily, Bedoo didn't need eyes. He relied on his nose and guided our driver to the main street where we found our friends waiting for us.

Now it was time to pay the drivers. Tarun and Neema started negotiating with them.

Neema thought the drivers were asking for too much money. She told us she wanted to pay half of what they were asking. Neema was a really good negotiator.

Within a few minutes she was able to agree with the drivers and paid them a fair price.

"It is two hundred rupees. That's the price of a rickshaw ride in the market," said the driver.

"My father told me the price of a rickshaw ride is less than that," Neema replied. "I know fifty rupees is a fair price for the ride, and since we used two rickshaws, I believe I should pay you one hundred rupees."

The driver realized that Neema was right and was happy to take her final offer.

Neema and Tarun told us that negotiating is very important in India.

"You should always know how much you're willing to pay before you buy anything," Neema said.

We were exhausted by late afternoon. We were ready for a nice meal. Tarun and Neema said we should eat right there in the market.

I was reluctant because the food wasn't familiar to me. My parents had tried to introduce Allie and me to Indian food before we left home, but we always got away with eating our regular favorite dishes.

Tarun told me that trying new things is always a good way to learn. He convinced me to taste a couple of colorful vegetarian dishes.

One was chole bhature, a chickpea stew with fried bread that looks like a big balloon.

Another was raj kachori, a crispy tortilla shell filled with lentils and potatoes drizzled with yogurt and mint sauce. Both dishes were delicious.

We even had some amazing desserts, including jalebi, a bright orange funnel cake soaked in sugary syrup, and my new favorite dessert, ras malai, a ricotta cheese dumpling soaked in sweetened milk and flavored with Indian spices.

CHAPTER IV

Diwali, The Festival of Lights

On our way home from school one day, Tarun told us about his and his sister's plans to celebrate Diwali, the festival of lights.

"Diwali is one of the most important festivals in India," he said.

"Why is it so important?" I asked.

"It symbolizes the triumph of good over evil or the victory of light over darkness," he said.

Tarun went on to explain the origins of Diwali.

"Diwali gets its name from the row of clay lamps that people light outside their houses to symbolize the inner light that protects them from all evil," he said. "The light from the lamps invite Lakshmi, the goddess of wealth, to come in to the house."

Allie and I listened to his story in fascination.

Neema described how everyone decorates their houses, their schools, and even their offices for Diwali, the same way we decorate for Christmas back home.

"Families get together to celebrate with food and especially with traditional Diwali sweets like jalebi," she said. "To represent the light, the city skies turn white from all the fireworks."

Tarun let out a big laugh. "It's so loud, but everyone has fun celebrating with their family and friends."

We were so excited when they invited us to celebrate Diwali at their house – and even more excited when our parents said yes.

All we did for the next two weeks was talk about Diwali. So much so that my parents were concerned we weren't focusing enough on our schoolwork.

To help us get ready, our mom took us to the market to get some special Diwali gifts for Tarun and Neema's family.

We learned it was customary to give your hosts a special present to celebrate Diwali. My mom bought them some very nice sweets and several clay lamps.

At last, Diwali day finally arrived! We couldn't wait to experience all the fun of the fireworks. Allie was wearing the new sari she had picked out with Neema.

As the sun went down, the fireworks got louder and louder and began to turn the sky white. We wanted to get a better view of the action, so Tarun and Neema took us to the rooftop of their building where we could see a large part of the city.

We spotted an amazing building, a very old monument our parents had told us about.

I remembered my mother had called it Qutub Minar. She said it was a minaret (tower) that had been built hundreds of years ago.

Tarun was proud to tell us more.

"Qutub Minar is the tallest minaret in India," he said. "Its construction began in 1192, and it is made of red sandstone and marble…"

We were once again fascinated by Tarun's story.

We laughed and played and saw the fireworks explode high in the sky until their white light made the city disappear in front of us. Neema was right! The sky turned completely white.

CHAPTER V

My Big Plan to Save a Wedding

Although we were having fun with the fire-works and all the sparklers, I noticed that Tarun seemed sad.

"Tarun, what's the matter with you?" I asked.

"Nothing," he replied.

But we could see that something was troubling him. We decided to try to make him happy. We competed to make the silliest face. No luck. Then we tried to tell the funniest joke. Still no luck.

Tarun didn't seem any happier for all our efforts.

"It's because of the wedding," he said.

Allie and I had no idea whose wedding, so we asked him to tell us more.

Tarun told us his older sister, Madhu, was getting married.

"Why would that make you sad?" Allie asked.

"My father's worried that we can't afford to give her the wedding she deserves. I want to help my family, but I just don't know how."

We tried to cheer Tarun up as he gave us more details about the wedding. We started brainstorming ideas to help him, but whatever we came up with sounded like it wouldn't work.

Finally, I thought of something. "I've got it, I've got it!" I yelled. "I've got the perfect idea."

"What is it? Tell us right now!" Neema said.

"Lemonade is my idea!"

"What about lemonade? How could that help?" Neema asked.

I went on to explain to her and her brother that in our country we sold lemonade in a little stand when we needed to raise funds for school or soccer or a charity.

"All we need to make lemonade is lemons, water, and sugar," I said.

"But we would also need a lot of thirsty people who want to drink our lemonade," Allie said.

Tarun laughed. "That's never a problem in India."

I came up with a plan for what we would need to do. "If we all help to make the lemonade, advertise it, and sell it," I said, "the cost of each glass of lemonade will be low and we'll make lots of money to help Tarun's father pay for the wedding."

"It's a good idea," Tarun said with a big smile.

Neema wasn't sure yet. "If we're going to make lemonade, then we have to make it really tasty," she said. "We need to add cumin and other spices and herbs so everyone will like it."

"Allie and I know how to make lemonade that everyone will like," I said.

We decided to share the responsibilities. Neema said she would provide the sugar and the water. Tarun said he would find the lemons. Allie and I said we would make the lemonade and an attractive stand for selling it.

But where would we sell our lemonade?

"I know just the place," Tarun said. "It's by the office tower near my dad's work in Connaught Place. Every day I see many people shopping at the stores. And a lot of people walk by to catch the bus or the rickshaws. Besides, Connaught Place is one of the most beautiful markets in the city. My teacher said it's a little touch of Britain in the heart of New Delhi."

"One more thing," Allie said. "We should all wear

a uniform – we should all wear a beautiful Indian outfit."

I wasn't too happy about having to wear an Indian kurta.

"I have a better idea," I said. "Let's all wear American clothes."

Tarun, Neema, and Allie looked concerned. They all thought wearing traditional Indian outfits would help us sell better. But they trusted I was making the right decision.

With our parents' help we gathered everything we needed: the sugar, the water, and, of course, the lemons … lots of lemons! Allie and I also worked really hard to make an attractive lemonade stand. It was all white with a few lemons drawn on it and the word "Lemonade" written in huge print.

Allie wanted to make the stand more colorful and even wanted to put some flowers around it. She thought people would find it more attractive because it would look more like their own outfits.

I listened to her, but said, "I like it white and clean. I'm sure everyone else will like that, too."

It was getting really late. We needed to get to bed so we would be well rested for our big day of selling lemonade.

CHAPTER VI

Spicing Up Our Recipe

Finally it was morning! After breakfast we met outside our building and hopped on an auto rickshaw for a short ride to the big office building near Connaught Place.

Tarun and Neema said they felt uncomfortable wearing their American outfits, but I assured them everyone would like how they looked.

With a crowd of people stopping to watch us, we put together our amazing stand and set the glasses and the lemonade on display for everyone to see.

But how much would we charge for a glass of lemonade? We didn't know. If we asked for too much money, no one would buy. But if we asked for

too little, we wouldn't make any profit and wouldn't be able to help our friends' dad pay for their sister's wedding.

"Well, people pay fifty rupees or more for a soda, and fifty rupees for a chai tea," Neema said. "So they can pay fifty rupees for our lemonade."

We trusted Neema's knowledge and agreed to charge fifty rupees. Allie ran over to the stand and wrote the price of a glass of lemonade for everyone to see.

Lots of people paused as they passed our stand, but none of them seemed interested in buying our lemonade. Only a few people did, and they didn't seem to like it very much.

"What's wrong?" I asked Neema and Tarun, who

had been talking to some customers.

"Well, they just don't like our lemonade," Neema said. "They say it's too sweet and lemony."

"But it's lemonade," I said. "It's supposed to be sweet and lemony. That's how we like it back home."

"Perhaps we need to change our lemonade recipe so everyone here likes it," Tarun said, and Neema

was quick to add, "In India we like spices, especially the taste of cumin, and herbs like mint and cilantro. I know just what to do. I'll follow Mom's recipe to fix the lemonade. I guarantee you everyone in India will like it."

"I agree with Neema," Tarun said. "Let's make some Indian lemonade."

I wasn't so sure about this change in plans until Allie chimed in with, "Neema and Tarun are right. Let's make Indian lemonade. We also have to decorate our stand to make it more colorful. Oh! And we need to wear our Indian outfits!"

The three of them looked so happy about the idea of Indian lemonade that I said, "Okay, I think you're right. Let's make it work. Let's have lots of fun selling our Indian lemonade!"

Tarun and Bedoo ran to the spice market to get the ingredients we needed. After they returned, Allie, Neema, and Tarun ran home and changed into traditional Indian outfits. When they got back, we redecorated the lemonade stand.

Instead of just sitting there hoping people would stop and buy the lemonade, Neema and Tarun advertised our lemonade by shouting to the crowds passing by, "Try the most delicious Indian lemonade ever made. Only fifty rupees!"

Even Bedoo got into the action, greeting everyone with a quick bark as they came over to purchase our new Indian lemonade.

So many people wanted our lemonade that Allie and I could hardly keep up. We served glass after glass until we ran out.

"Everyone loved the Indian lemonade!" I shouted. "Everyone loved the Indian lemonade!"

Neema and Tarun were really happy I had listened to their ideas. Allie was happy she got to wear her new sari and learn more about Indian culture. Bedoo was happy he got to bark all day without anyone telling him to stop.

Best of all, because everyone helped in making,

selling, and advertising the lemonade, we were able to make a lot of profit to help Tarun's father pay for the wedding. Tarun couldn't wait to tell his father. He knew he would be very proud.

"Get ready to attend the most amazing Indian wedding ever!" Tarun told Allie and me.

"Yes," Neema said. "You are invited to our sister's wedding!"

CHAPTER VII

Madhu's Wedding Day

I didn't know what to wear for the wedding. I was curious about trying on a kurta pajama with the traditional shoes, but I wasn't sure if I would feel comfortable wearing one.

Allie, of course, was very sure she would wear a green- and gold-colored sari she had tried on at the market a few weeks earlier.

As we headed to the market to look for clothes, Allie said, "Let's try on a lot of beautiful outfits. We'll look amazing, and most importantly, we'll look like everyone else."

I still wasn't sure, but Allie went on with, "So far I love everything about Indian culture. The colorful saris make me feel at home with everyone."

It didn't take much for Allie to convince me to try on and purchase my first kurta pajama.

It wasn't bad. It was actually very comfortable, and I was able to find a color I really liked. I was so glad I tried one on. With a new sari for Allie and

the nice kurta pajama for me, we were finally ready for the wedding.

The wedding was very different from weddings we had attended back home.

The groom came to the ceremony on a horse followed by a huge procession of his family and friends who chanted and danced to very loud and cheerful music played by drummers.

The bride awaited the groom inside the big wedding complex with Neema, Tarun, and all her family. According to Allie – Neema had snuck her back for a peek at her sister – Madhu was the most beautiful bride she had ever seen.

"Madhu is wearing the world's most beautiful sari," Allie said. "It's made of red fabric and has been decorated with thousands of colorful, shiny stones."

After the groom came in to meet the bride, all the guests formed a long line so they could greet them and wish them well. Our parents joined us when it was our turn to congratulate the groom and the bride.

It was an amazing party. The decorations were colorful, and the food was great. I couldn't stop eating ras malai!

Everyone had a wonderful time meeting people. Allie and I joined Neema and Tarun and danced to the sound of Indian music until our parents told us it was time to go home. They were proud of us for helping Neema and Tarun make this wedding possible.

CHAPTER VIII

On to New Adventures

I'm so happy we had the chance to spend time in New Delhi with our parents. Allie and I learned a lot about this beautiful city and about India. Our main teachers were our friends Neema and Tarun, who helped us adapt to the culture.

I'm really looking forward to returning to India some day. But for now, my family and I are getting ready to fly to our next new home far away from home.

In a few hours we'll be on our way to another amazing destination!

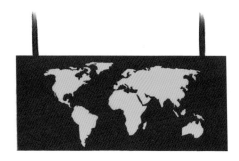

Rocky's Diary of Incredible India

India is an incredible country.

It has a dizzying variety of cultures, landscapes, and traditions. It is a very large country, not only in size but also in the number of its inhabitants.

India is home to more than a billion people. Its residents make up sixteen percent of the world's population. That is roughly four times the population of the United States. It is surpassed only by China in the number of its inhabitants.

Geographically, India is about one-third the size of the U.S. It is the seventh largest country in the world. Its amazing array of landscapes includes verdant tropical rainforests, sky-high mountain ranges, vast deserts, and incredible seashores.

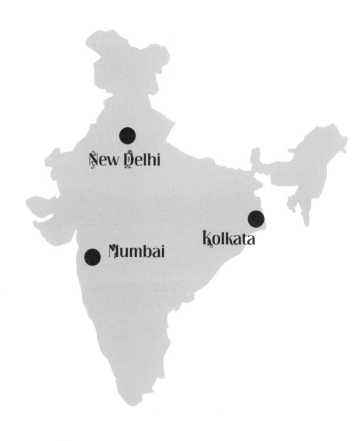

Discover India

Official Name: Republic of India (the official name in Hindi is Bharat).

National Symbols: The Tiger (animal), the Peacock (bird), the Lotus (flower), the Banyan Tree or Fig Tree (tree), the Mango (fruit), and Cricket (sport).

THE CITY OF NEW DELHI

New Delhi, the capital city of India, is located in the larger metropolitan area of Delhi and is one of eleven districts that form the National Capital Region (NCR). New Delhi was officially declared the capital of independent India in 1947.

Delhi is a diverse city that combines the old and the new in harmony. Old Delhi is full of rich Islamic architecture, labyrinths of narrow lanes that now host popular markets, forts and castles that protected the city from invaders, and formidable mosques and monuments from the Mughal era.

The total population of Delhi's metropolitan area is approximately 22,800,000. It is the largest metropolitan area in India, and one of the largest in the world. Delhi has roughly the same number of people as the entire country of Australia!

The sari is the national dress for the women of India. A sari is a long strip of fabric, usually cotton or silk, that varies in length from four to nine meters. In its most common style, the sari is wrapped around the waist creating a skirt, and then wrapped around the torso and over the shoulder baring the midriff. A petticoat and a blouse are also used with a sari.

A kurta pajama is a traditional form of clothing that consists of two pieces: a kurta and pajama pants. The kurta is a loose, long-sleeved shirt that is knee-length. The pajama is loosely fitted; it is drawn tightly at the waist and tapers at the ankles. A simple kurta is a perfect outfit for everyday life, whereas a more decorated kurta can be used for formal events.

Who Were the Mughals?

The first Mughal emperor was Babur, a descendant of central Asian warlords. Babur invaded northern India in 1526 and established a powerful empire called the Mughal Empire. This new empire would remain for more than 300 years.

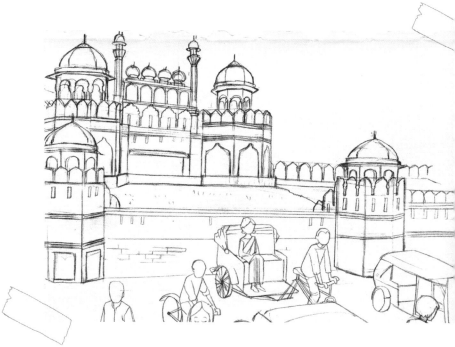

The Mughals were Muslims who ruled a country with a large Hindu majority. The Mughal leaders allowed Hindus to reach senior government or military positions. New Hindu temples were built with their permission. The Mughals also believed in the importance of education, art, and science. During their rule in northern India, the region enjoyed peace and prosperity. They strived to build unity and stability within their empire.

The Mughal Empire began its decline when leaders decided to persecute the Hindus and attempted to convert them to Islam, or to convert them to Sikhism, a new religion that blended many beliefs of the Muslims with those of the Hindus.

As a result, the Hindus began to rebel against their Mughal rulers. In 1858, the leaders were completely overthrown, which ended the Mughal Empire.

NEEMA'S RECIPE FOR LEMONADE

SPICED INDIAN LEMONADE (JAL JEERA)

Ingredients:

3 cups of ice water

1 tablespoon ground cumin

1 teaspoon mint leave paste

2 tablespoons lemon juice

½ teaspoon kala namak (kala namak is black salt from the Himalayas)

1 pinch of sugar

½ teaspoon amchur powder (The spice amchur is made from unripe or green mango fruits that have been sliced and sun dried)

½ teaspoon ground coriander (optional)

Mix well and serve chilled with ice. Garnish with mint leaves.

Published in 2013 by
Adventures Nation
Calgary, Alberta, Canada
http://adventuresnation.com

CPSIA information can be obtained
at www.ICGtesting.com
Printed in the USA
LVIC070258060713
341681LV00002B

* 9 7 8 0 9 9 1 9 6 1 9 0 0 *